Getting Through Your First Year in Network Marketing

Getting Through Your First Year in Network Marketing

Table Of Contents

Foreword

Among the great things about making cash on the net is that returning cash from net marketing is something that's available to everybody. It doesn't matter whether you've a college degree or not, and unlike most jobs, past experience isn't necessary either.

A different thing that makes net marketing such an attractive choice if you're seeking a way to make cash is that contrary to most offline business choices you may name, you don't need a big chunk of revenue to launch an net business either.

This doesn't imply that cash doesn't help, or that there's no cost affiliated with net marketing. To the contrary, if you've some cash to invest in your business, it may quicken your journey towards success by a substantial margin but if there's no cash available, you may still accomplish success as long as you're willing to put the time and effort in.

When a person first gets moving in net marketing, they are by definition a beginner, somebody who's simply started their net marketing career. In net marketing idiom, they are a 'newbie', somebody who's simply learning the ropes.

When you're still at the net marketing fledgling stage, it may be hard as there are a lot of distractions and pitfalls that may get in your way. As a matter of fact, there are so many likely errors and things that may miscarry that it's broadly agreed that of the individuals who decide to make cash online, more than 95% will never get anyplace whereas less than 5% will make cash and accomplish some degree of success.

Therefore, it's fair to suggest that it's in no way a given that if you decide you wish to take in cash from the net that you'll do so. Indeed, the bare stats suggest very much the reverse as highlighted above.

So, the focus of this book is really firmly fixed on how you move past the fledgling stage of net marketing without falling foul of the many pitfalls and hurdles that may easily derail your nascent net-based money marketing job.

Here you're going to learn about the errors that so many newbies fall foul of to prevent them accomplishing success and how you may avoid doing the same.

Will this assure your success? Woefully, likely not because there are so many variables that ultimately decide whether you're successful or not, and not all of them are controllable. For instance, as with each situation in life, being in the correct place at the correct time may have a huge impact on how successful you are and this isn't truly something that you've any control over.

But here's the matter. If you know what the errors to avoid are, you may avoid making them. If you're witting of how you take your business to the next level, you may do so. Both of these factors better your chances of accomplishing success by a huge margin, and after reading this book, you'll have a clear understanding of what these errors are and how you may prevent them.

Surviving Your First Year In Network Marketing

The Ultimate Defense Against Attrition, Burn Out And Competition In Network Marketing.

Chapter 1:

The Biggest Error

Synopsis

In my experience, likely the biggest single issue that net marketing fledglings have when they decide to attempt marketing or making cash on the net is that they come at this business from totally the wrong angle or position.

Whilst a few individuals who have previous business experience approach the concept of working at the net in the same way as they approached their prior business ventures, the vast majority don't. It's therefore no coincidence that these individuals are commonly the ones who are most likely to bomb.

Let me 'paint' a fairly common scenario so that you may see why this occurs.

Individuals who begin trying to earn cash online for the first time do so because they require additional cash. Whether this is because they have to replace the income that they have lost as a result of a job loss or whether it's to yield a supplemental revenue to pay for holidays, better Christmas gifts for the youngsters or whatever, the fact is, they need cash.

A Mistake

Now, let me say directly that if you discover yourself in the same state of affairs, there's nothing per se wrong with turning to the net to yield the extra money that you need. Indeed, as pointed out in the institution, there are so many benefits to running a net-based business that if you don't have any other more obvious lucrative opportunities available, utilizing the net to generate additional revenue makes a lot of sense.

However, coming at the notion of making cash from the net with no other parameters, guideposts or controls than a vague belief that you'd like to make some extra cash is an almost sure recipe for calamity for one simple reason.

The lucrative side of the net is a veritable jungle inhabited by thousands of different products all competing for your attention and your cash.

Every one of these products will brazenly proclaim that they're the key that you require if you're to unlock your net fortune. Additionally, a lot of them will make ridiculous, bizarre claims about the amount of cash you may make that will inevitably turn the head of an net marketing fledgling who sees these claims for the first time.

The fact is, there are 100s of net marketing products which range in caliber and effectiveness from being outstanding to horrifying. And naturally, as a net marketing beginner, it's inconceivable to sort the wheat from the chaff without spending cash on products like these.

It's therefore all too easy to make expensive errors that mean that you end up spending cash on the net, instead of earning it.

Wasting cash in this way (unavoidable as it might be) is an error that will derail your marketing career before it's even got decently started.

You consequently need to think long and hard before you start spending cash, as once you have got the mental side of net marketing crystallized, the rest becomes relatively aboveboard.

The beginning thing that you have to do is to identify precisely what it is that inspires you, or what it is that's driving you to run your own net business. As suggested earlier in this chapter, it might be because your career has gone so you've no choice or it may be to put extra money in the bank for the luxuries of life like foreign vacations, a new car or even a new house.

Whatever it is, you have to identify this 'driver' as each and every day when you're actively involved in running your business, you have to keep this motivational component in the forefront of your brain as this enables you to remain motivated and centered.

As a matter of fact, what I'd advocate is that if the motivation behind your business activities is something that may be pictured, then why not add a picture of whatever it is that's driving you to the wall behind your monitor or on the whiteboard that you utilize for business planning?

For instance, if its better vacations that you're working toward; why not place exotic beach scene pictures in a place where you can't avoid seeing them each morning or evening when you begin work? If its

toys for the children's Christmas Day, utilize family pictures of
Christmases past for precisely the same purpose.

This helps as regardless how thorough your business plan is, you can't
anticipate or foresee each possible eventuality. The unforeseen will
occur (e.g. you're half way through creating a video and your
computer crashes) and when it does, it's often exceedingly frustrating
and irritating.

Bearing the motivation in your clear line of sight will help you get
over those times when it may be a bit hard to keep going as it won't
allow you to forget what got you began in the first place.

Chapter 2:

How You See Your Business

Synopsis

Many marketers decide that they require extra cash and that the net is as good a place as any to yield the additional income that they require.

But simply having a vague notion that taking in some extra cash from the net may be nice idea isn't the basis for beginning a business. And, whether you've realized it or not, if you're going to market on the net in an effort to yield additional money, then what you're doing is running a business, nothing more and nothing less.

Now, realizing that marketing net is a true business might not seem really crucial but it is in fact a vital notion to accept on board. If you don't accept and comprehend this and approach your net marketing activities as a hobby or interest, you've directly made it endlessly harder to accomplish success.

Trying to make cash from the net is a serious business and ought to be treated per se. It is not a hobby or pastime, as if you treat it as a hobby, then what you wish get in return for your work is a hobby level revenue.

Even if you're running your net marketing business on a half-time basis, it makes no difference. It's a business and must be treated as such from the very start.

How You See It

It's utterly vital that you comprehend and follow this apparently simple guideline as if you do so, you'll set yourself apart from the majority of would-be net marketing millionaires who merely don't get it. If all the same you treat your net marketing actions as a hobby or pastime, then the chances of accomplishing success are almost zilch for lots of different reasons.

Consider it this way. If you were assembling a business in your local shopping center, you wouldn't treat that as a sideline or interest, nor would you go into it with nothing more than some faint idea about 'making cash'. After all, arranging a business of this sort is going to cost you many thousands of dollars, so naturally you'd take the whole thing real, very seriously.

All right, so when you arrange a net marketing business, you don't need to spend 1000s of dollars on getting going. Nevertheless, that doesn't alter the fact that it's still a genuine business in precisely the same way that it would be if you open a store in the shopping center. When you accept that what you're doing when you begin generating a net income is running a business, then an awful lot of additional factors ought to fall into place pretty much directly.

When you comprehend that your net marketing actions constitute a true business, the next step ought to be obvious. There's no successful business on the face of planet that's ever accomplished success without having a business plan in place, and there's no reason to expect that you may buck the trend by trying to run your net business without having such a plan in place.

Now, the thing here is that before you may put such a business plan in place, the beginning thing that you have to know is how you're going to make revenue. And deciding how you're going to gain revenue on the net is a different hurdle or pitfall that will frequently cause issues for a newbie who is not yet really sure of what they're doing.

The issue here is that there's simply too much choice. There are gobs of different ways of making cash from the net, and 1000s of products that at least in principle teach you how to do so.

The issue is that a lot of these products are contradictory, as they frequently relate the writers or creators own personal techniques of making revenue on the net. Whilst this means that presuming that the product creator is telling the truth, you may follow their techniques and make revenue, this isn't always the case.

Moreover, as there are so many different products available a lot of which tell a different story, it may become incredibly confusing if you're attempting to find a way of making revenue that suits you.

Take as an illustration the idea of making cash by selling 'stuff' on eBay. Given that this is the world's number 1 auction site, you'd think that making cash by selling something on eBay would be relatively aboveboard and that there would be a reasonably widely agreed, standardized process for making cash doing so. If however you search Google for something like 'make cash from eBay', you'll discover that there's an awful lot of data available with over seven a half million results indexed.

Take a look at any of the eBay results brought back and you'll discover the big amount of data and advice, but a lot of this advice will seem to be contradictory. Consequently, it's very hard to know to do for the best.

Because there is so much data available, many fresh net marketers suffer what is known as 'analysis paralysis', or an excess of data in other words. As they've too much data available, they get confused as to what works and what doesn't, with the outcome that they do nothing because they're scared of making the wrong selections.

This issue is exacerbated by the fact that most fledgling marketers are occasionally a bit gullible when it comes to net marketing products. As a outcome, many individuals who have just began marketing on the net seem to have complete trust that the next 'latest and greatest' product is the one that they've been waiting for, the one that's finally going to shoot them to net marketing superstardom.

As an illustration, they may see an info product that promises to show them how they can make $9,000 a day utilizing Google AdSense, so they purchase it.

They study it and maybe they begin to put into action the plan about which they've just read. If so, the chances are that they'll not stick with it very long as they wish to begin making money fast and this particular way of doing so doesn't appear to be working for them.

And naturally, they've already signed up for the e-zines of all of the big names in the industry, so a few days later, data about the next wonder product, the one that's utterly guaranteed to make their fortune, arrives in their e-mail inbox. And naturally, they purchase it and try it, only to discover that they make no more cash with this product than they were with the prior one, therefore they cast it away and purchase something else that's a 'assured winner'.

It's incredibly typical for net marketing newbies to jump from one product to a different in this way. As they get sucked in by the hype, it's all too simple for them to trust that the latest product on the market is the one that they have to have, so they purchase product after product in a ceaseless search for something that truly doesn't exist, and naturally they waste a huge sum of money in their futile search.

And equally obviously, whilst they're jumping from product to product, they're not centering their efforts and attention on merely one business plan or technique, which further deepens the calamity. So, having painted a fairly blue picture of what you shouldn't be doing, now let me provide you an idea of what you ought to do.

The beginning thing is to do a little research so that you may make an informed decision about the sort of online business that you're going to run with. Whether this is making revenue from eBay, affiliate marketing, producing niche targeted blogs that you monetize with AdSense or whatever, you have to choose one business model and stick to it.

What you're seeking is a step-by-step guide to doing one thing well, because if you may discover a business strategy that's proven to work and stick with it, you'll make revenue. Once you've a technique that you're going to utilize, you're almost ready to begin producing your business plan, but not quite as there's still one crucial factor that you have to crystallize before pressing ahead.

Chapter 3:

Synopsis

If you've an idea of what sort of business you wish to begin with, you have to likewise set objectives or targets for that business.

Without having an objective or a target, your business activities are inescapably going to be unfocused and random as if you don't recognize where you're going with your business, you've no chance of attaining an acceptable destination.

You wouldn't depart on a trip in your auto tomorrow without knowing where you're going and either knowing how you arrive there or at least having a map or a navigation system to help you do so.

Well, attempting to run a business without having any clue of what you wish to accomplish is precisely the same as departing with no clue where you're going and no clue about how to arrive there.

Now naturally, you wish to as much revenue as possible from the net as fast as you may, but this isn't an objective or target. You have to specify how much revenue you wish to bring in and set a time scale in which you wish to accomplish that aspiration or hit that target.

Your Direction

On the other hand, what you must prevent is setting unrealistic or overambitious targets that you've no realistic chance of accomplishing. Irrespective of whether the sales page for the 'how to' product that you have simply bought tells you that you are able to make 1000s of dollars each day utilizing this particular lucrative business model, you can't, or at any rate, you shouldn't anticipate to begin earning a fortune immediately.

Be truthful with your target, and read around the net about the specific business technique that you're considering following to get a thought of how much money you're likely to make. This is crucial because it helps you to have a truthful estimate of what you are able to expect to bring in, which in turn helps you to establish accomplishable objectives.

As an illustration, if you are going to produce a niche targeted blog web site that will be monetized with AdSense, this is a web site that you are able to realistically expect to generate $50-200 a month as long as you set it up properly. Therefore, if you are able to set up one a week (which should not be too hard), then after 6 months, you would have twenty-six niche targeted web sites generating $1300 a month or more.

This may not seem a great deal of revenue, but remember that this is money you're generating without having to sell anything and naturally, a few of your niche blogs are likely to yield considerably more than $50, so the real figure is likely to be greater. All the same, it gives you a realistic ball-park figure to begin with as an objective or minimum target.

Synopsis

To carry on with this illustration, if you recognize that your objective is to build twenty-six niche targeted blog sites over the beginning 6 months of your net marketing career, then you may start formulating your business plan by working backwards from this to found precisely what you have to do to hit the target.

To produce your business plan, I'd first recommend that you utilize either a whiteboard, a really big sheet of paper or mind-mapping software like Freemind to produce your plan.

The reason that you ought to utilize one of these resources to produce a business plan is that by doing so, you may add different business thoughts to the 'plan' in a relatively random manner instead of in a sequential way as you would if you were writing things down line by line on a sheet of paper. This lets you 'group' objects together as necessary once you're satisfied that you've everything noted on your plan which makes the whole planning process more consistent.

Your Road Map

When you're ready to begin planning, you have to brainstorm the questions that you have to address.

For example, if you are going to produce twenty-six niche-targeted blogs, are they all going to be in the same market or in dissimilar markets? If for instance you had a series of blogs that were all centered on the weight loss market, this may be appropriate in terms of linking every blog to the others and it may make things simpler if you were to become an authority on one topic instead of being somebody who tries to get by with twenty-six blogs that center on totally dissimilar markets.

How are you going to come across enough niche ideas to produce your blogs? Utilizing resources like eBay Pulse, Amazon.com, Yahoo! Answers and 43 Things will help you to muster up a list of things that individuals are searching for on the net, but what specific aspect of these interests should you produce blogs for?

You've already decided that you wish to monetize your site with AdSense but how are you going to drive targeted visitors to your blogs? Without targeted visitors, you're not going to make any revenue, so this is an essential question to address.

One way that you are able to publicize your blogs is by issuing articles on major article directory sites like EzineArticles or GoArticles but if you're going to do so, are you going to author the articles yourself or will you get somebody else to do it for you?

What about the articles that you post on your blogs? Where are those going to come from as each of your sites will require at least 6 unique articles, so do you have the time and the aptitude to author them or not?

Videos are a excellent way of publicizing your activities, with 1000000s of individuals visiting leading video networking sites like YouTube , Google video , Daily Motion and MetaCafe daily. Therefore, if you can publish video content that's centered on the same niche as your blogs, you are able to get a ton of free visitors, so it's definitely something you ought to do.

To do so, you require video ideas and the equipment and/or resources essential to make these videos.

Do the ideas you have demand utilizing a digital camcorder, and if so, do you have such equipment or can you afford to purchase it? If on the other hand your videos are going to boast 'action' that may be recorded from your computer display, you don't have to purchase anything as you may utilize free recoding software like CamStudio.

As you'll find out if you have not already, there are virtually 100s of different ways you may drive targeted visitors to your web site, and each time you come across a fresh traffic generation technique, you ought to add it to your business plan 'chart' or mind map.

This is why you ought to utilize a resource like a whiteboard or mind mapping software where you may add fresh data in a seemingly random manner as all of your new traffic ideas need to be grouped together into a total traffic generation sub-plan.

You ought to likewise have a content creation sub-plan and so on till you've all necessary parts of your business plan gathered.

If you search the net, you may discover lots of places where there are free business plan samples available. Frequently, these business plans are complex and really wordy, primarily because most are business plans that are mainly designed for handing out to potential business investors.

If you're in a position where you're attempting to invite outside investment into your net business, producing an equally detailed business plan of this sort may have some value. However, assuming that the business plan you're producing is only for your own use, it makes far more sense to keep it easy and straightforward instead of making it overly complex and lengthy.

To continue with an earlier analogy, what you have is a roadmap that gets you from point 'A' to point 'B', not a high-definition atlas of each country on the face of the earth.

The simpler and more aboveboard you can keep your plan, the better your plan is likely to be as simplicity makes it far easier to center on the most crucial aspects of what you're doing as there is little or no clutter to distract you from your primary targets.

Chapter 5:

One Step Further

Synopsis

Having a well thought out and comprehensive business plan is something that you utterly must have if you don't intend to stay at the bottom of the web business hierarchy forever. However, having a plan isn't adequate on its own as it is not the plan that runs your business or takes action, it's you.

Therefore, once you've identified precisely what your motivation for attempting to make cash online is, established objectives that will delineate success for you and created a business plan that will let you accomplish those objectives, you have to introduce particular personal qualities to the mix to make the whole thing occur.

The beginning thing that you require is determination, as without this characteristic, it's all too easy to quit at the first sign of trouble or frustration. Regrettably, however, it's a lack of determination and a willingness to do whatever is essential to make things work that leads so many marketers to leap from one product to a different without ever giving any one idea adequate time and effort to accomplish success.

A Broad View

Once you've decided upon the specific business model that you wish to abide by, its determination or willpower that will to a big extent dictate how successful you're going to be.

You have to accept from the beginning that there will beyond question be times when things don't go the way you wish as this is what occurs in everything you ever do in your life.

However if at the very first sign of troubles, you merely quit and decide to try something else as this particular idea obviously doesn't work, you're never going to give any single business technique enough time to be successful.

On top of determination, you require doggedness plus both the ability and willingness to put in the essential hard work.

In spite of what you may read elsewhere, running an net business is no easier or harder than running any other sort of business, and you wouldn't expect to begin your own haulage business, Law practice or meat market and be able to get away without putting in a little time and work.

Precisely the same requirement for work and effort applies to running a net-based business too. It's exceedingly crucial to have the power to remain centered and to ignore distractions. And in the same vein, it's likewise critical that you comprehend the importance of prioritized what needs to be done so that you may identify what are the true essentials of running your business and what are distractions.

For instance, a lot of marketers leave net chat utilities like MSN or Yahoo! Messenger permanently enabled so that individuals may contact them immediately. Don't be tempted to do this, but it serves no purpose. The truth of the matter is, 99.9% of the time it is not essential to have instant chat utilities open as all they do most of the time is distract you from the primary jobs on which you ought to be focused.

In a similar manner, while it may occasionally serve a purpose, you ought to avoid spending all your time on forum sites and in chat rooms even if these sites are based on the niche in which you're promoting.

Whilst there are a few situations where forums are useful, participating for the sake of doing so is a distraction, one that may consume many hours daily.

Submitting a constant stream of updated Tweets on Twitter is a different fun activity that may consume excessive amounts of time without you ever even recognizing it.

Focus is utterly essential as assuming that you've only a certain number of hours daily to dedicate to your net business activities, you have to utilize that time as profitably as possible.
For this reason, I'd advise that at the beginning of each week, you list down everything that has to be accomplished during that week.

Then, group everything on your list together as logically as conceivable before allocating a particular day where everything in a specific group has to be dealt with.

I'd advocate that you then finesse your timetabling still further by switching the two hardest, unpleasant or obstinate tasks to the top of your list so that they're the first 2 (or 3) jobs that have to be accomplished. If you get the hardest or unpleasant jobs out of the way first, then everything else that you have to accomplish gets relatively easy and aboveboard, hence the reason for organizing your daily calendar in that way.

At the end of each work session, you ought to hopefully have marked off each job on the daily list as being accomplished. However, because the only thing that you may ever rely on 100% is the unforeseen, there will be times when you don't get everything on your list completed on the day you specify.

In that situation, I'd still recommend that you deal with the most obnoxious tasks on the next daily worksheet first before going back to the unfinished projects from yesterday.

And naturally, on those days when everything goes perfectly and you're in fact ahead of schedule, it adds up to begin dealing with the next day's work a day early.

But, in that situation, leave the task table topping hard jobs till tomorrow and instead center on some relatively aboveboard tasks, as you've already dealt with today's 'toughies' and 2 or 3 hard jobs is enough for anybody in one day.

The final thing that you ought to bring to the net marketing table is a sense of fun and adventure. While I've stressed on a lot of occasions that marketing online is a serious business, it doesn't necessarily follow that it has to be a business which isn't amusing or enjoyable.

When you truly know what you're doing, you ought to find that the whole thing is fun, something that feels more like a pastime than it feels like work.

This is excellent as if something is fun and perhaps a little exciting; it's far easier to remain enthusiastic about what you're doing. In turn, exuberance means that you'll do whatever has to be done far more effectively and efficiently than you would if it was a difficult slog for you. Therefore, you ought to try not to forget how crucial it is to make the whole net marketing venture as much fun and as exciting as possible.

Naturally, for most of us who market online, the true excitement comes when you begin seeing cash land in your PayPal or Clickbank account, and there's no doubt that once the cash begins rolling in, it's far simpler to keep your motivation levels elevated.

Chapter 6:

Synopsis

I've already suggested that there's a vast amount of data about making cash on the net out there in the market and that this flood of information may frequently be more harmful than it is helpful.

And the fact is that if you're like most individuals who have just began or are about to begin their own net marketing business, you're likely doing so on your own, so faced with this massive data mountain, it's really easy to become befuddled, distracted or ambushed.

For this reason, it might add up to attempt to find somebody with whom you may work and from whom you may learn. There are a few different ways you may do this, with the better option for you likely being dependent on how much experience you have and where you are in your net marketing career at the minute.

If you're somebody who's already mastered particular basic net marketing skills, your knowledge allied to any previous experience that you've already adopted means you've an asset, albeit an intangible one. In net marketing, possibly more than in any other business environment, knowledge and experience represent true assets and if you've an asset, you've something that other marketers will put a value on.

Take A Good Look

What this means is, if you've something valuable to bring to the table, you may seek joint-venture partners with whom you may work.

When net marketers arrange joint-venture partnerships, the common idea is that each member of that partnership bring something valuable to the table which the other partners can't bring, and has suggested, with experience and knowledge under your belt, you've an asset to provide likely partners.

To discover individuals with whom you may 'team up' in this way shouldn't be particularly hard either. For example, the first place I'd seek suitable partners would be the chief forum sites in the niche in which you're operating.

In a JV operation, you and your partner (or partners) would all be equals in the project, but for this to occur, you have to have some skill or ability to bring to the partnership table.

If you don't as yet bear these skills or powers, your situation is somewhat different. In that case, what you ought to be looking for is a teacher or mentor instead of a partner. What you truly require is somebody from whom you may learn, somebody who will train you from the ground up so that you learn everything that you have to know from an authority.

There are a lot of ways that you may find individuals who would be willing to and capable of mentoring or teaching you everything you have to know about net marketing. But remember, you have to learn from somebody who truly knows what they're doing so you may learn the stuff that truly matters whilst avoiding the distractions.

Therefore, finding a mentor is basically a two-stage process, as you first need to find somebody, and second you have to verify that they've the ability or experience to give you what you require.

The 1st strategy for finding someone who may genuinely teach you what you have to know is to do so is through the leading forum sites in your market sector. Running an aboveboard Google search for forums in your niche will show you which are the most popular, as they'll be the ones at the top of the search results page.

More often than not, if you are able to find a forum site that's obviously the leader in your market sector or niche, you'll find that most of the 'big names' in your industry will participate in that forum. These individuals are unlikely to be regular contributors, primarily because they abide by the advice that I gave you earlier about avoiding spending too much of your time on bulletin board sites.

After all , the 'big guns' of net marketing are too busy earning millions of dollars yearly through their net-based business activities to spend hours daily on a forum.

Nevertheless, it's a fact that even the top boys in the industry will contribute to the leading forum sites in your market sector from time to time, and all you need to do is to spot who they are.

Luckily, this isn't especially difficult, as other members of the forum will commonly point you in the right direction if you watch what is going on closely enough.

To take this concept a step further, suppose that by utilizing this method, you've discovered somebody who's obviously an authority in your market, a well-known expert in your niche.

Quite clearly, you can't simply come straight out to ask this individual to help you. After all, they don't know you from Adam and till you've done a lot more background research on them, you don't know whether the business idea that you're thinking about adopting will place you in direct rivalry with them or not.

Therefore, once you've found person, you have to do your background research to discover as much as you can about them. In addition to establishing whether you're going to be in direct rivalry with them or not, this research may help to uncover a few more highly cogent factors.

First, it will let you build a broad picture of their business interests, experience and skills. This ought to help to clarify whether they're the sort of individual you ought to be approaching for assistance or not. Having this background will also make a difference when you first approach them for their help.

The 2nd thing that you might discover is that they may already have some sort of mentoring or training materials available, meaning that rather than having to approach them directly to ask for help, you may sign up for their program or product instead.

The point to remember here is that the individuals who have reached the top of the tree in your industry have done so for a reason. Essentially, they had a well thought out, professionally developed business plan which they followed with determination and total focus so that they accomplished what they set out to accomplish.

So, there must be a second option because if 'plan A' doesn't work, you must have an alternative 'plan B'.

In this case, the 2nd option is to look at sites that are centered on finding mentors for individuals who need them. This Canadian site <http://www.mentors.ca/findamentor.html> lists dozens of sites where you ought to be able to find a suitable mentor with whom you may work and from whom you may learn, so I'd definitely recommend that you take a look.

Consequently, if you think that having a mentor will help you and you can't find anybody suitable through your own efforts on the leading forum sites in your niche, this is a great site to begin your search for a valid 'plan B' option.

Chapter 7:

Keep Your Cash

Synopsis

As I advised earlier, there are virtually 1000s of products out there that purport to teach you how to yield cash from the net. There are a fistful that are really good but the huge majority are not worth wasting the paper to print them out.

Regrettably, I know this as over the years, I've managed to spend money on a very small number of products that really justified the price and lots that were garbage. But here's the thing.

If you're an net marketing newbie and you wish to move beyond this stage, there truly is no need to get your charge card out of your wallet as everything that you really need is available free of charge!

Moreover, you've already seen the resource where all of this top quality marketing data is available at no cost because I'm discussing the Warrior Forum again here.

There are naturally many forums that center on net marketing but although I've visited and utilized others from time to time, the only forum where I can truthfully say that the info available is always top notch is the Warrior Forum.

Consequently, even if you can't find a suitable mentor through the site, what you may find is lots of top quality info from some of the best-known names in the online marketing business.

Forums and Products

The point about these guys isn't so much that they are well-known names but that they're recognized authorities, expert figures who may always be trusted to present precise info whenever they post on the forum. And as this is a forum that has been around a while, a place where many less well known but equally competent marketers gather, it's a literal goldmine of the sort of info that you need to take your net marketing career to the next level.

And regardless what sort of info you're seeking; the chances are that with a little patience, you'll discover everything that you require on the Warrior Forum site.
There's one other thought about spending money that you may want to take into account too.

Many of the 'how to make cash online' products that you may eventually purchase through sites like Clickbank are 'test marketed' through the Warrior Special Offers (WSO) sub-forum of the primary site.

When this occurs, you always get a special deal on the product being offered so it pays to keep your eyes open for fresh product offers of this sort. Not only do you know that most individuals who sell through the Warrior are commonly pretty good at what they do (they've a reputation to protect on the best-known net marketing site); you'll get their products for a fraction of the true value.

As I advised, it really isn't that necessary to spend cash but if you're going to do so, take a look at the WSO page before putting your hand in your pocket.

Chapter 8:

Taking It Farther

Synopsis

In a like manner to the business mentor idea, you are able to utilize a site like the Warrior Forum to discover a business model that works, one that really has the potential to earn 1000s of dollars a month.

But the thing to comprehend here is, don't ignore the age-old proverb about not attempting to run before you're adept at walking! Put differently, there are dozens of different business ideas available free of charge all over the net but you have to pick something that you may honestly do.

Don't let yourself be blinded by the cash angle here either. There are lots of business themes that have the truthful potential of generating a lot of cash but you have to consider your own skill set and abilities before diving into something that's totally unknown to you. For instance, if you've spent your net marketing career to this point making cash from niche-targeted blogs that feature AdSense, you've already learned that the key to making cash with a site like this is your ability to yield targeted traffic.

Therefore, assuming that you've already enjoyed a degree of success, you've discovered how to yield targeted visitors for a site. Hence, the question now is, how may you apply that knowledge to make more cash than you're currently yielding?

Ramping It Up

As an illustration, in the same way that yielding cash from an AdSense monetized blog is all about your power to send targeted visitors to the site, successful affiliate marketing is likewise predicated on the same power or skill. It might therefore be that you may transplant your traffic generation skills and techniques by switching them to affiliate marketing to make more cash than you're currently earning.

To accomplish this, you've a choice of paying for a product where the creator has a vested interest in convincing you that it works or you may find something free where the creator of the theme has absolutely no financial interest in convincing you one way or the other. Rather obviously, in the latter scenario, you're far more likely to get the truth or the real picture, so wherever conceivable, this is the way to go. It's a fact that regardless what market you decide to operate in or the business model you select , there are already 1000s of individuals in that market doing pretty much what you're planning to do.

If you decide that you're going to become an affiliate marketer, you're likely number 5 billion on the roster of individuals who have made the same conclusion. Moreover, it's a fact that of those people, 4.9 billion have already quit the business as they didn't make it and while you might be totally confident that you're different, the fact that so many individuals have failed before ought to provide food for thought. In a perfect world, you would be able to examine what they did wrong so that you may prevent making the same errors yourself. Regrettably, it is not a perfect world and you don't have the capacity to discover precisely why most individuals didn't make it whereas a relatively small fistful of marketers did, so you have to adopt another approach.

What you need to do is come up with an 'angle' or a unparalleled selling point that makes your business different to those operated by others who are doing a similar thing to you on the net. For example, if you're acting as an affiliate for a Clickbank product and it's a popular product, you already know that there are 100s if not 1000s of other affiliates promoting the same product, a lot of who will be doing so in precisely the same way if you don't have your own unparalleled approach. What you therefore have to do is come up with an angle or something that you may 'brag' about as it makes you stick out from the crowd.

As an illustration, most affiliate marketers are lazy so they market the product they're supporting by linking directly to the original product creators sales page in all of their promotions. This approach has its attractions as direct linking will yield maximum sales as it puts the minimum number of hurdles all roadblocks between the prospect becoming aware of the offer and the point where they place their hand in their pocket to find their billfold.

Even so, if each affiliate marketer is doing the same, then it's impossible for each of those people to differentiate themselves, meaning that the choice of affiliate link to follow in effect becomes a lottery. If however you provide some sort of added value to the offer, you increase the chances that you're going to be the one who lands the sale. For instance, rather than sending the interested prospect directly to the sales page, you may send them to your own 'bonus offer' landing page where they're presented with a superb bonus package merely for signing up through your link instead of through another persons.

For the buyer, this represents an enormous deal as they were going to purchase the product anyway but now they get a truckload of additional bonuses too.

And for you, this technique represents a double winner, as not only does it add a fresh customer to your business, it likewise enables you to collect e-mail data from that fresh buyer in a way which you'd never normally do as an affiliate. This occurs because in order to get their bonuses, you ought to make it clear on your bonus offer landing page that they have to send proof of purchase through your link by e-mail to claim.

The bottom line here is, you have to do something that's different enough to stick out. If you are able to be unique and memorable at the same time, you build your uniqueness and a power to think differently which automatically makes you stick out from the herd.

Without a unique angle or selling point, you're just one very small fish swimming in the same direction as every other occupied of a really big pond.

In this book, I've emphasized again and again that you shouldn't waste revenue on products that are not going to take your business forward. This doesn't however imply that you shouldn't invest in your business when the time is right to do so as investing in yourself is one the most effective and fastest ways of taking your business to the next level.

For instance, if you've previously utilized article marketing to promote your business, you likely realize that writing and publishing articles on the major directory sites like EzineArticles is an exceedingly effective marketing technique. Even so, although utilizing articles to market your business is extremely effective, you likely also know that sitting down to author articles is a relatively time-consuming activity too.

Therefore, when you've enough cash coming through the door to justify it, you ought to spend a little cash on hiring others to produce your article marketing content for you.

After all, a 500 word article that's perfect for external publication will cost you someplace between $5 and $10 but that investment will save you half an hour or maybe even an hour which is time that you may utilize far more effectively and profitably in other ways.
In a similar manner, whenever you hit a barrier that may most effectively and efficiently be overcome utilizing a paid tool or resource, you ought to give very serious consideration to spending the cash necessary to capitalize on that resource.

As a simple illustration, if you wish to build an e-zine, then you need an auto responder system, and the most effective and profitable autoresponder systems cost money. Don't look at money spent on a resource like a top quality autoresponder as an expense, viewing the outlay rather as an investment in your business and future profitability.

Again, try looking outside the immediate parameters of what you're doing at the moment by adopting a 'big picture' aspect of where your business is at the minute to have a clear-cut idea of how you ought to allocate capital in the future to develop your business further.

While it ought to be clear that I don't urge wasting money on products or services you can't utilize in your business immediately, there are decidedly times when you have to invest in your own business and future. And if for instance it's something that you are 'definitely going to require in the future', forget it as by the time your future becomes a reality, the system will already have been 'upgraded', so disregard it.

Once you're ready to take your business to the next level, it's going to be necessary to place some investment into what you're doing.

While I am not necessarily speaking about 1000s of dollars, if you wish to move from being a net business beginner to being somebody who's considered an intermediate level marketer, you have to have all of the tools and resources in place to warrant this 'upgrade', and that necessitates spending some cash.

It doesn't truly matter if you're still running your business on your own from your back bedroom, it's in many ways far more crucial that your image is correct, and to a large extent, you accomplish this by investing cash in your business.

Wrapping Up

As you ought to hopefully comprehend by now, getting beyond the newcomer stage of net marketing isn't anywhere near as hard as some people may imagine it would be.

All that's truly necessary to step up to the next level is to adopt a more professional, businesslike attitude to your net marketing actions, and everything else will fall into place almost mechanically.

Many net marketers seem to feel that marketing on the net is somehow a fresh sort of business, one where you may afford to be far more casual and laid-back than you may in traditional 'real life' business.

And while there's a degree of truth in this - you don't have to commute or wear a collar and tie for instance - to believe that net marketing is a completely different sort of business is an error.

Marketing and selling on the net is precisely the same as marketing and selling in your local shopping center, and the disciplines that you'd need to apply if you're running that sort of business are precisely the same too.

For instance, it's essential that you're organized and that know what you're going to do every time you fire up your PC in advance of doing so. You have to stick to both your 'big picture' business plan and your daily schedule as nearly as possible, and when a task needs to be done, you must make certain that it gets done either through your own work or because you arrange for somebody else to handle the task.

Most especially, if you don't want to be a fledgling forever, you likely need to rethink how you're operating your business on a daily basis.

If you're not already adopting a thoroughly businesslike, professional attitude as highlighted in this book, you have to begin doing so and even if you're already relatively businesslike, you need to 'up the ante' by becoming a bit more of the ultimate net marketing professional with each passing day.

It's not hard and it may be accomplished, but the only individual who can take you from being a newbie to being somebody who's enjoying a great deal of net marketing success is you.

Now you know how to accomplish it, it is time to begin making whatever changes are essential to take your business and your net earnings to the next level.